Wizdome's Poetical Therapy

A Collection of Self Discovery Poetry
and Insightful Poems

Angela Winston

BookLeaf
Publishing
India | USA | UK

Made with ❤ on the BookLeaf Publishing Platform
www.bookleafpub.in
www.bookleafpub.com

Dedication

This book is dedicated to my Mom Carolyn Sanders and Dad Henry Johnson who believed in me before I could even speak and told me I would be heard. I did it again Momma and Daddy...

Rest In Eternal Peace

Acknowledgement

I'd like to take this moment in time to thank my Husband Toriano and our sons De'Angeleo and De'Jevone. Guys, you have given me the strength I needed when I was weak and I am eternally grateful for the indulgence, I truly appreciate all the love and support you've given me over the years. That love I treasure and send back to you tenfold.

To my Sisters, Sistahs, and my day ones that hold the titles > S.I.S (you know who you are) and to my tight knit circle enclosed in steel, you guys are appreciated more than you know!

Preface

The poems in this collection are the results of many years of active listening and internal reflection that lead to self rediscovery. It has been a journey that has given me the ability to express myself fully and freely. Hoping it does the same to you as you read the words within this book.

Reflections of an Internal Storm

In the mist, I'm so blind, couldn't
see it coming, you insidiously aiming
for me...

Dragging me down into the very belly
of the storm...

At times you gave me unimaginable
pain...

So much I couldn't see, the deviousness
behind you making me believe....
No beauty resides within me...

Self-respect, I used to have that,
Where did it go I cannot recollect,
at this time I don't know because
the reflection I see doesn't show...

But now I've become wiser,
I became stronger and

in the mist of the storm,
a beauty was born.
Can't you see it's falling like rain
down my face leaving an invisible
trace,
I'll take the blame for loving you so
deep, so true...
Now in a dream state unable to
believe we're through...

No you can't feel the pain in my heart,
like a monstrous beast tearing
me apart...

Wretched claws ripping into me, never
stopping until my poor heart is
shredded beyond recognition....

The last vision of you distorted as it
bleeds out ...

No attention was given to the tears
I've cried throughout the years,
Hidden in the depths, you never saw
me shrink within myself, becoming

half of who I was meant to
be...

Can't you see it?

You never really saw me so busy seeing
what you wanted to see who you
wanted me to be, so you missed it
when I began to grow, becoming wiser
day by day...

This was a reflection of the storm raging
within me....

After the storms rage, we become wiser,
We become smarter, and the radiant light
shines upon you eventually, you come out
on top...

Stop allowing those who are unworthy of you
to define who you
are...

A Vision in a Storm....

Who is SHE

As I weep, I weep deep down inside,
therein lies the pain, locked where no
one resides, no one to interrupt the
uncanny peace of a broken individual...

Who is she ....

Who fixes the one who fixes others,
who puts the puzzle piece in place

that's missing for puzzle champion...

As I weep, deep inside, hiding the pieces
that no one can find...

The one who appears to be unbroken...

Is she me...

The one that knows she is to be the
blessing to everyone else, selfless
love; the ability to give to someone else,
but at what price must she pay, she'll
just put it in a box for another day...

The one that appears to be unbroken...

Who is she...

Disillusioned by many, so it's easy to cut ties,
her tolerance for bullshit you cannot find...

Is she me...

Smile that smile, dance that dance, solve the problem,
take the chance, build that bridge, pass that test, save
everyone, yet fail at saving, saving herself...

The one that appears to be unbroken...

Is she me...

The one that appears to be transparent yet is opaque, layer upon layer of the protective shell
that's put in place, is she hiding from herself?
If so what piece has been defaced...

Hard to understand, do you see what I mean...

Who is she... is she me?

The one that appears to be unbroken...

The invisible door that is wide open yet
shut, she's the one you turn to when you

get stuck in a rut, what lies within is so
thick akin to the fog, to see is unseeing
you blink and it's gone....

Who is she...

Who is staring back from the mirror, the
image
is unclear, indistinct; almost as if it's glazed
over
by the steam, of a shower that was never on,
never to be seen...

Is she me...

The life of a party with no one in attendance,
the
beater of a non-existing drum, she is the
leader of
a marching band that has no band, a one
army
woman at her own back she'll stand...

The one that appears to be unbroken...

Trust has never been an issue, because
it is rarely given...

The question is given...

Who is SHE ???

The good, the bad, and the ugly with all
that entails...

UNEQUIVOCALLY,
UNAPOLOGETICALLY

SHE. IS. ME

What Is It To Be a Woman

Is it the gender bestowed upon me at birth?
Is it this that ties me to my own self worth?

Is it the features etched upon my face, the
hair upon my head? My eyes, my lips or my
sex that has society trying to put me in
my place...

Is it my breasts, hips, or what lay between
my thighs? Is it my size? Or once again....
my sex that part of me that identifies me
as ...

A WOMAN..

It is my womb, the uterus placed within?
My ability to create a human life?
Is it my choice to bring or deny life upon
this earth, bearing what could be seen as
a gift or curse, the ability to give...

Birth?

Is it their choice to give or take away?
Is it the right for men even to have a say?
Am I not a woman?
Is this not my body ?
Is my voice so redundant that these
be the very reason my choice is taken away?

I refuse to be cowed, afraid of being punished
for what I have to say! the demoralization
shown
of my position let's me know you never
respected
me as a woman anyway...

Yet this only shows the character of the
person
you are, which has no bearing on me, it's just
sad
that not even this you can see...

So YOU can NEVER tell me what it is to be
a...
woman in this

Society ...

Letter To Every Woman

Being everything to everyone is tiring,
just waiting for someone to see you for
who you are and not what you can do
for them at the detriment of losing you...

Getting up in the morning to putting on
your wonder woman's cape, making sure
the kids are clean,dressed and they ate
the food on their plate ...

Making sure your mate is straight and
mentally all right, sometimes tiptoeing
on eggshells to prevent an argument
or fight...

Getting dressed looking perfect for work,
doing additional jobs, keeping busy to hide
the hurt, the desolation, even the emptiness
felt inside, after all you're so good at hiding in
plain sight when cornered with nowhere to
go,
and nowhere to hide ...

It's not the only image we can accept, yet
this is the one we seem to cling to, hit rewind
and do it all over again...

Now, there's nothing wrong with taking care
of
home but...

Where do they end and the NEW You begin...

What will you do with and for YOU when
THEY
are all gone...

Forever lost... Or Found..

Oblivious to the fact that the protective barriers
I was subconsciously building were blinding and
robbing me of life...

Lost sight of hope, of life, I got lost in the world and
forgot about me, so you'll have to Forgive me for not
being able to show you the way it would be, like the
blind leading the blind as the old folks say...

Coulda, woulda, shoulda, don't mean a thing, they're
just regrets stuck on rewind while wasting YOUR time....

As they say EVERY rose has a thorn,

before they cut them off, does that mean you
ignore the
rose for something you can't see or will you
choose to embrace
that one good thing...

Life has scales to balance the good and the
bad, don't
waste life on what will never once again be,
because what
was lost was meant to be...

Lost or found...

Pivot, readjust as it will become a new
beginning.....

Or never more until you see the final ending...
Chose to win or lose

Do you understand what I'm trying to say...

Or is it still simmering...

UnLeashed

How many times have I been broken? How many times!
It seems too many to count, disregarded, set aside,
unable to see any way out...

Crawling because I didn't have the strength to stand
Unable to see that the disparities of life was getting
the best of me, I had actually lost my identity and trying
to find me according to society's standards....

Yet the label of that angry black woman when injustice
is pointed out, or a disagreement is had then your touted
as being aggressive, because passivity is the accepted way
they teach a lesson!

Ha! Imagine that...

Labeled as weak if in hard times, you have nothing to say,
because you're always supposed to pick a side, even when
you have no dog in the fight...

When the world is wrong and you're the only
one standing
up for what is right, hypocrisy at its best,
wouldn't you agree?
because you want me on your side when
you've already
labeled me!

Vitro is spewed when disrespect is not
accepted, daily veiled,
and sly remarks that have been allowed to
slide with the turn of
back or roll of an eye...

Wrong accepted as right and right proven as
wrong with a slight
of the hand, while protected as if it's right!
how long is it expected
or allowed to go on; this distorted reality that
I'm supposed to
survive as if this was the 1800s all over again..

You really have me twisted!

The vitriol that is spewed on a daily via social
media, world news,
even Google has people confused! You can
continue to test me if
you want to...

Now I no longer care what you think about
my eyes, my nose, my
lips, the melanin in my skin or my hair! Hell
you get surgery to be the
mirror image that you try so hard to break...

I'm taking back what's mine—Mind, Body
and Soul, I will no longer allow
Society to have any type of control over the
being that is me!

Tired of being tired, sick of unnecessarily
being sick, societies, trying to
slightly revert back to the old days, sublimely
changing mindsets that the
old ways are really where they were, the lies
they tell and get away with is like
an Edgar Allan Poe novel with a twist...

The political arena is a joke! Throwing the rock, but hiding your hand! you
tell the lie and never take stand, remove the laws of protection, put in
place, all in the guise of making this world a better place, you poke the bear,
yet expected it not to react, so busy trying to trap the mouse your hand gets
snapped in the trap!

Are you ready? Are you really prepared to face the diabolical person that you
have created the aforementioned actions? Are you prepared to face what
you have in actuality .....

UNLEASHED?

Could be you ...

It's definitely

ME....

Chasing

No longer chasing people, you know
those that pretend to be your friends...

Just for you to find out that they're your
friends alright...

Fair weather friends indeed, in the end...

No longer chasing what seems to
be impossibilities, nah, got no time
for that, it's such a precious commodity...

No longer chasing the unattainable,
that glass ceiling means nothing to
me, I've busted that out, it is now
a past vestige to me...

No longer chasing if only, coulda,
woulda, shouldas' those heffas
would only hold me back, an unlikely
Lot, I have no desire to go looking back...

No longer chasing my dreams cause I'm
making those come true...

Now's the time to decide if *that*
something in your life is worth chasing...

Ask yourself...

Are you chasing it or will it be chasing...

You....

Screams from Within

The feeling of hands being tied
with an invisible rope, it's like
having a crack pipe with no dope...

Having an umbrella with no chance
of rain, having no heart, yet still able
to feel pain...

Anxiety on what happens next
The difficulty of someone who
needs to be checked...

Refusing to see the trap that lay
waiting inside, trying to see out
of blind eyes, cries falling upon
deaf ears...

No one to hear the lonely cries
A bound mind seeking answers
it may never find ...

Where's your choice...
Find your voice...

Life's Trenches

I'm going to put on my clothes and tell
the story of how I made it through
In order to get over—

Look...

Life will put you in its trenches, It will try to get it's hold on you and it won't let go, It will drag you down if you let It, and It'll take everything away if you don't have yourself grounded, you've got to play for high stakes...

When you get situated, try if you can, to find a little bit of peace and once you do, better hold it close, lock it away, then protect it because life's a beast...

Listen ...

Don't let the naysayers get in your head, learn when to walk away and bury them in your memory as if they were just passing through, makes it easier for 'em to become dead to you...

Learn ...

Life doesn't pull its punches, so why should you? and it will kick you in a ditch–leave you drowning in the trenches, because life can be a...

Bitch...

What?

Is this untrue...

Life... The Greatest Gift

Life is to be lived, it's one of the greatest
gifts that God were able to give, although the
road was at times tumultuous, just think
you still live in his grace, so take a moment
Smell the flowers, because no one is promised
the next second, minute or hour or day...

LIFE...

I don't really know what to do, I don't really
know what to say, all I know is the proof in
how I live my life each day, no one can tell
me how to live, well how to live my own life
because I've had to grow from my Struggles
and My Strife...

At times life has knocked me down, it made
me
even want to give up, I had to do what I had
to
do, and at times I didn't give a fuck, had to
find

my own reasons to live when I was down in
the
dirt, had to get on my knees, then I had to get
right back up and get to work...

LIFE...

Took a moment to learn from the lessons
given in
the past, there's a reason for those, just take a
deep
breath and ask–what is your purpose? and
then make
a choice to live each moment! to use your
voice, Live—
to leave a legacy so they'll remember your
name, live
for yourself, then your children—that's really
the name
of this game...

Some that are buried 6 feet deep would want
to be in
your place, so take a moment and think of
how you really

want to LIVE the rest of your life, in this time
and in this
space...

When staring in the eyes of death, will you
wish for...

L.I.F.E?

Conversation with Self

You've got to accept the good with the bad,
realizing
what you never had, you can't give up on me
and I
won't on you, learning to accept me with all
my faults
and all my truths...

Every day won't be sunshine, there will come
rain, for
every laugh and smile know that there will be
pain, most
beauty has some ugly underneath, what comes
next
depends on what you seek...

Start watching and pay close attention, hear
what others
say, not what you wanna hear, you'll see
things become
clear, yet the conflict comes when you see
what people

do, however oftentimes what they don't do
sometimes
matters more than they'll ever know, see you
can't
continue to show up for others and while
showing up for yourself too...

You'll catch that later.. or not—if you
continue to hide from the truth...

Stop, unintentionally, blocking your
blessings, It's time to
focus on you, in order to find yourself, you
must accept things
as they are and stop hiding from truths that
are hidden and
buried, take note because a lot of fake friends
and dreams
are in that cemetery...

The Battlefield

You've won the battle but who'll win the war? You never know just what life has in store....

You take and take yet have nothing to give, it's like how to survive vs how to live...

Who have you chosen to be on your

team? Respect, loyalty, and trust today
is all a dream...

You think you've won but it's all in your
mind trying to find balance in such a
hectic life ...

Life's a battle, do you choose to run or
fight? What will you choose in this thing
called life...

So much experience, yet still wet
behind the ears, you don't even
know how to fight, still in a battle
with
your
own

fears...

My Mind

I'm feeling overburdened, my heart is still, it's
hurting,
my mind can't seem to take the pain ....

My mind is overwhelmed, I don't know how
to swim
but, I have hope that Jesus is here again, in my
mind
it's shattered and broken and in mind my
heart is out
of tune, in my heart I can't hear what is
spoken,
because I'm shattered and I'm broken, cause
I'm
shattered and broken....

I'm feeling so darn helpless, I can't even help
myself
'cause my mind ain't even in tune, I know it's
overwhelming
and millions are just like me but they don't
know you like I

do 'cause in my mind I'm hurting, my heart
feels so burdened,
How can I shove it all aside?

I try and I try, my mask is in place the only
thing I need to
do is get up on that stage, but my mind is
shattered and broken,
and my feet, they can't reach the stage and the
steps they look
so far away...

Can I stay in this dark place...

Can I stay in this dark space?

Motherhood

More than JUST a Mother

We have birthed nations, we have birthed
Kings
and Queens, Presidents come from a
Mother...

We have built kingdoms upon kingdoms, put
stakes
down to create villages, villages upon which
you
lay your head ...

We are more than just mothers...

All of this work stems from what is called...

MOTHERHOOD...

The most important job in the world, being
in charge

of the future for the next generation, it's a
thankless
job, but with the best payoff you could ever
ask for...

Sacrifices are made day in, and day out, there
are lessons
learned you'll never forget but in the end...

It's all worth it, it truly is, if you take the time
to get it right—that
is...

It comes with having to think for more than
yourself, having
to take into consideration somebody else, a
child, a whole nother
human being, in the beginning, you get
nervous, you get sweaty,
you panic, not knowing what to do, or to
think...

But then you get the hang of it, and it flows
becoming second
nature for some...

Motherhood...

What a blessing indeed, hard to believe this
job was given to me...

It doesn't come with an instruction manual, it
doesn't come with sound
advice, it doesn't always come with the
instinct to nurture, but it does
come with struggle and strife ...

It comes with late nights and early mornings,
adjusting to the sunset and
the sunrise it comes with knowing that you're
blessed with such a sweet
surprise...

Motherhood...

I have been truly blessed to have mothered
children that I can call my own,
children who love me unconditionally and
accept me for me, and I can tell
you that is a blessing indeed...

Motherhood....

I
Wouldn't

Change

A

Thing...

Sensual Reality

No worries. It's just me and you, in
the mirror by candlelight, silk and
lace against my skin all night...

Ummhmm...

This is just where we begin...

Looking sexy while I'm staring in your
eyes, with you sizing' me up cause I'm
looking just right...

Oh baby, touch me, tease me, yes,
I know you need me, baby, I look
innocent, but looks can be so very
deceiving...

Ummmhmmm, yes you need these
thick lips, hips, and thighs, slow it
down a bit as the temperature in this
room is on the rise...

Oh yes...

Baby I'll relax as your hands are
sliding down the silk lingerie, while
it lies around my hips, as I sway, from
side to side, while I'm imagining that
you're all mine...

As you whisper sweet nothings sensually
into my ear, saying all the things you know
I want to hear.

So let me be that NovaCain alleviating
painful
thoughts from your brain....

Yet, I must ask, can you do the same...

Oh yes, say my name....

Sensual Whispers...

Let's play a game...

The Process

The flower I picked for you today
as you were on my mind, thinking
of all the things you did, and all
the things you'd say, it took me
back in time...

A time when life was simple,
honest, and true, the times when
you resided here on earth and I
could be with you...

It represents the deep abiding love
that I know you had for me along with
you pushing me to never give up, as
eventually you knew I'd succeed ...

The flower represents the rebirth of the
wisdom you instilled within me, making
me wise enough to understand that your
life had to end in order for you to gain the
peace you so rightfully deserved and was
desperately in need...

I picked a flower for you today, and yes
indeed
the process gave me a wiser outlook
on things I never knew I was in need to see...

Trust the Process...

Distorted Reality

I should be dreaming, because this can't be
real, this
world we now live in, don't know how to feel,
walking
around suppressed, depressed and we still
don't know
the deal ...

Why can't truth be on the table, while all we
hear are
lies, walking around with heads in the sand
then we just
don't realize we're putting our life in the
hands of those
who really don't care, to talk about the next
bill to pass,
to line the pockets of bureaucrats...

The government is hiding things, CNN don't
know what it
brings, one day we're fine, then the next we
don't know

what's going on, sitting waiting on a check, a check that's
not based on reality! the lives of you and me, well they're
putting us in a box, watching as we're getting knocked off...

Selling dreams as solutions while the world is still so full of
pollution, and they wonder why we're here today! so many
gone so many passed away, disrespecting what we were
given we don't even understand how we're living...

It appears they have their heads in the clouds while the
government, it is livin' out loud, while we are made to
Suffer, after all, they have the best healthcare, better than any other...

They can still comfortably take care of their families, while

here we are in reality losing jobs, we're losing
loved ones it hits close to home but they don't
see because
they're livin' in a distorted reality like the
Twilight Zone...

Can you believe what you see? I think Not !
only half of what
you see is real, and believe only half the
falsehoods wrapped
in truth as they whisper in your ear, they'll
have you think seeing
is hearing and hearing is thinking, have you so
discombobulated
half the time not knowing how to feel..

Standing and staring at this Oak tree, when's
the last time you
were able to come and see me ...

Is this a dream? This world can't be real, what
I'm feeling you'll
know the deal yet the way the world is set up,
I'm wondering
when are you gonna see...

Me.....

I guess

I'm....

Living in a distorted reality

The CROSSROADS

It's disappointing when you realize that
the very pedestal you've built and placed
someone upon, that same someone is
mentally busting yours apart, it's also
when you come to the realization they
are human and their feet are made of
clay...

One must realize the vision God has
given to you and the path you should
go, is just that...

Your vision and your path,
when you accept that, you must
also decide what you will sacrifice
to make your dream a reality...

The greatest mistake ever made
is becoming so comfortable with
anyone that you become dependent
upon them, you lose sight of yourself
thus relinquishing your very

independence...

Promises made yet forgotten,
thus broken, resentment eases its
way in blocking honest communication,
so that when conversation enters the
picture, you hide your wants, needs,
and passions...

A sure pathway for disaster as when this
happens the foundation you built everything
on implodes....

Yet once a decision is made you must
stand firm on it, or all will be forever lost
leaving you at...

The CROSSROADS...

New Beginnings

I have succeeded even when I thought I'd fail,
been
through the fires, literally sat in hell, played
devils

advocate with my life as the debate, dedicated myself
to love, had to walk away from self sabotage and hate...

Criticized myself at every turn, everything that made me,
ME made the fire burn, even my creativity didn't feel a part
of me...

About gave up! Was at my wit's end, work, life and kids almost
did me in ...

Life got to the point where I didn't know up from down, I thought
life is never going to be easy, but damn I never thought it'd be
this hard I had to get my kneepads out, bow down and go
hard, harder than ever before...

I had to go to God no matter what the world would say, it always

comes against me anyway, got knocked down
10 times, yet got
right back up, I'm still winning even though
the pressure of this
life wants to keep me stuck in its loop...

I almost allowed it to do me in, I had to prove
myself TO myself
time and time again, had to take my own
thoughts and words into
consideration, to myself I gave a new
DEDICATION...

No longer would I allow myself to be thrown
out or tossed about,
just to be the topic in situations giving a free
demonstration regarding
a simulation of what not to do in this game
called life...

Lost a lot of my battles both literally and
figuratively in this worldly and spiritual
game, I couldn't see I'd come to be blessed
mentally, physically and verbally

armed to the teeth, now fully equipped to
face life in the valley of its beasts...

I guess you could say ....

I wrote the score ....

CHECKMATE !

I. AM. WOMAN.

Now...

HEAR. ME. ROAR.

A Moment In Time

The moment you realize you are more than
what
you've become, the more you realize, that you
are
becoming the next version of you...

A moment in time...

You've put yourself on a shelf, taken food out
of your own
mouth for others, be it mentally, physically or
emotionally,
you've taken from your own being, you've
taken and given
your essence away without a thought of where
you
would be in the end...

A moment in time...

The moment you realize you've been turning
your
back on yourself, you've been sleeping on
you...

it's time to wake up ...

That moment in time ...

The moment that you realize you've put
yourself on a shelf,

you've allowed life to pass you by, letting your
gifts go to waste...

You've unknowingly put your life in stasis
Become complacent, unaccepting of the
greatness that lie within...

Will you continue to waste away minutes,
seconds, hours in days?
In essence throwing the blessings you've been
given away...

The hands of time move forward, never to
turn back, if this should
be your last moment would it be full of
regrets?

What are you waiting for?

You only have one life to live—

This is THAT moment in time...

SEIZE IT...

The Removal

Let go of those
Who don't respect you,
Who don't support your dreams,
Who hold you back,
Who purposely mislead you,
Who continue withholding facts
that will control outcomes...

Know what I mean...

Walk away from those who drain
you emotionally, physically, and
most importantly spiritually....

Stop giving power to those
who want to control your moods
as if they're thermostats in a room,
as it creates a toxic cycle, you owe
them nothing...

There shouldn't be a cost to just being
YOU...

Understand that you owe yourself
everything! including a piece of mind
before you can demand these things
from someone else you must first
demand them of yourself....

Your relationship with yourself is
most important, choose to love
yourself, selfishly and watch the
tides turn....

There's value in being...

YOU!

The Perfection of Deception... The SmilE

Smile to show pure joy
Smile to mask the weight placed on
your shoulders ...

Smile when you feel like the world is over
Smile to take the heat off unspoken
words...

Smile to show that you are strong
Smile to hide what's really going on
Smile a perfect way to mask the pain,
which behind the eyes will remain ...

Smile to hide the deception from the world
Smile to wash over the fake and polite
rudeness society often gives...

Smile for self preservation masking the anger
that resides within...

Smile making a silent statement, they can
never
see you sweat
Smile so one ever sees what comes next...

Smile, an overpowering, nonverbal
psychological
weapon of warfare that you never thought to
use...

How do you wield this weapon...

Such a perfect weapon of deception....

The Smile...

ReSumption of Self

Sometimes I have to remind myself that
everything starts within the mind; see
the Lord removes obstacles out of your
way every day, before you even pray, he's
got you, however, are you accepting of this
at times unprayed for ...

Gift....

Stay safe, protect your mind and thoughts,
these
remain blessed in your space, your place, your
sacred space wherever that may be...

How do you just be? accept the grace given
with
no reprieve, can it be disregarded to put your
self
at ease, that is the question that poses itself to
me....

This feeling is pushing towards
problem–solving and
resourcefulness rather than focusing on the
negatives,
this empowers you to channel inner energy
thus finding
creative solutions and turning your
restrictions into
stepping stones towards progress, the trials
you face today
have the potential to transform into blessings
...

Turning your ship into a masterpiece....

Each challenge has the ability to shape you,
inspire you,
and bring out the best in you, will you allow
life to overtake
you, or will you overtake it...

Take a deep breath, embrace the storm, and
unleash the
creativity that resides within....

Never let your Self Rediscovery...

End...

Internal War

Oh, how I rejoice that you are no longer in pain, that you are not suffering needlessly....

I also know my heart is hurting at
the moment, it's a pain that has yet
to heal, I know you know the pain
I'm feeling because at one point
here on earth, I was yours and
you were mine...

I know you can see the tracks the
tears made after they've made
the journey from my eyes down my
face...

Seems I must embrace the reality
that comes to me because I cannot
refute the facts that year after year
and day by day my heart hurts, but
the knowledge remains that you are
now in a better place...

In a forever land, land with the streets,
paved with gold and you're embraced by
the Lord ...

But still, yet my heart is hurting, my very

being aches for an embrace that I'll never feel again, a whisper that I'll never hear again, a phone call that will never be answered and a visit that I'll never again receive...

Still yet I'm hurting, yearning for yesterdays that will never turn into tomorrows ...

It's a conundrum in the least...

The battle of pain that lay within the battle for peace...

The Evolution ... Of Me

For so long I've taken everything you
dished out and got lost within myself,
put everything on the back burner,
even my freedom was put on a shelf
as I thought of you and nothing else...

I always put you first...

The intricate web you wove around
my mind and inside my heart had
me so wrapped up in you I was so
blind to your faults, I was so confused...

I always put you first—

I wake up and think of you even as
I'm battered and bruised, but I guess
it's OK this time, you left no marks on
my face this time, only a space in my
heart that's void, as my feelings
become numb to the pain, I guess
in my convoluted thought process...

And this is love? Say it again...

Still, I always put you first—

Peace of mind gone, Self-respect no
longer exists, put on the shelf, a dusty
one at that, I couldn't find myself, there
was no looking back, a murky existence,
no clear skies in sight, no profound existence,
no longer had the will to fight...

Yet again...

I always put you first...

But never again no more...

Peace of mind I'll find that bitch, Self-respect
I'm digging her out that ditch, that shelf! I'm
knocking the damn thing down, that murky
existence, to find myself well I'm climbing
over
clouds because I've found the light...

The "she" that I used to be, before you
thought to
destroy me...

As you continued to put me down hit after
hit, kick
after kick, vicious words, inhumane thoughts,
for
her I'll look high and low, I'll drag her from
the pits
of hell...

For...

You no longer have control of my mind, body,
or
soul...

I've taken back my Crown...

I'll no longer put you first...

Ashes to ashes dust to dust, buried that
passive chick,

that was must, for my eyes are no longer
wide-open
shut...

For a country that cannot see the value of
the...

Black Woman, a Black Queen...

For those that want to utilize violence and
verbal abuse
to enslave the momentarily weak...

For those that cannot see the true unspoken
strength
that lies within the silent being that is me, the
me I've
finally set free...

I'm now putting HER peace, FIRST....

This
is
the
EVOLUTION

of

ME....

Acceptance of Self

Everybody wants to rule your world...

The question I pose is, will you let them?

Will you allow them to break you, belittle
your efforts, needlessly waste your time...

Will you accept yourself with all your flaws
as you come to the realization that what the
world deems as Imperfections, is what makes
you who you are...

Unknowingly, you have been annoyingly
perfecting
a flawless heart...

When will you remove the veil from your eyes
to see
that you really are the beauty within the
mess...

Will you allow them to have you
second-guessing yourself,
have you on rewind trying to redefine your
perfection

that is disguised to the world as
imperfections?

A dichotomy of scars masked by tattoos
unknowingly aware
they will forever remain as soul marks
surrounding your
heart...

All wrapped in the beautifully and
imperfectly, perfect
package that you are...

God knows what he's doing, who are they to
judge?

Jane Doe

That dead place, a part of you that has died, that barren, desolate place inside that has withered...

She's in a place unknown to self, let alone the world, the worlds are so unparalleled to what she has gone through, where she has been mentally, spiritually, and emotionally hidden to the world....

She...had...to....Go

She had to be put away permanently buried, so that YOU could re-emerge into your purpose...

It had to be...

She had to die so that you were able to see through the residual damage that was wrought upon you unknowingly...

That being, was destined for a purpose that she never knew would be the catalyst of the rest of her days...

She leaves behind the legacy you must consciously and subconsciously reject,

to reign in the domain you were
placed in to complete the assignment in
which you find your purpose ....

Jane Doe....

It's time to let go of the trauma so that you
can finally...

TRIUMPH...

The REBEL

Never one to fit in or be satiated by what is
the
expected norm, am facing the facts of reality,
I've always been rebel born...

Standing up for what is right, dictated by MY
beliefs, not the watered-down version you try
to force feed, me...

Make up on or a bare-naked face, my natural
given beauty can never be erased, as well as
whether my hair is bone straight, kinky, or
curly,
hmmm make it a twist I'll always be ME and
only
I can adjust it...

My rules, My way...

Accepted or rejected, I'm not the societal
norm,

usually, the quiet observer with the ability to
bring
the storm, coming out smelling like guns and
roses
knowing I'm the chosen one, because I'm
blessed,
protected, you could say I AM Godly
approved...

Cross me if you want too...

I live by my rules, let society adjust...

Clarity is given so that I'm not
misunderstood...

As a Public service announcement this is a
must
so your internal thermostat or the social
temperature
of room can adjust...

My rules, my way...

So, make the decision or draw a line in the
sand in the
end, be clear with your intentions when
dealing with
me, you should know and understand, love
you but
I don't need you...

Born to be a rebel, I even withstand the
storms ....

For I know that I am ...

REBEL BORN

The Manifestation of a Dream

Reality and perception are rarely in
sync with what we want, and what
we really need isn't always what
we think...

At times we believe we can go through it
alone
trials and tribulations will give you an
uppercut that will knock you down,
but it's up to you if you want to get
back up...

Or... Not

When you get lost and confused or
suddenly lose sight of the dreams
that's when depth and clarity of the
mission are thrown off track and
nothing is as it seems...

To believe takes courage, it takes

action, it takes a whisper, to spear
it in the atmosphere, to do this you
must relinquish all doubts and release
all fear....

Dreaming is easy, but do you have
what it takes to make them come
true...

It takes getting out of the comfort
zone you've for so long made your
home, it takes hitting the underground
scene, down deep in the dirt saturated
in sweat and yes at times silent tears
when you didn't win that competition,
when you didn't get that deal ...

It takes trust that things will fall into
place, when it's your time to take center
stage, cause that's what it takes to get
there...

This is what happens with...

The Manifestation of a Dream...

Dreams To Reality

Grind and hustle, Hustle and grind

It's remaining turned up when you're turned down, going to bed at the crack of dawn 'cause you can't sleep til you finish layin' the melody or beat for that last track to the song...

Hearing music in your head, believing that one day those tunes gonna get you fed, until then...

Grind and hustle, Hustle and grind

Hearing your favorite DJ on the radio and dreaming one day they're gonna be playin' me with my songs on that show, yeah just wait and see cause one day I'll be able to say "it was all a dream"

Until then...

Grind and hustle, Hustle and grind

Getting that call and happy as hell,
yet at the same time so scared you'll
fail, but suck it up cause you had to...

Grind and hustle, Hustle and grind

Knowing that you gave your all to
this game...

You'll do just fine....

Suppression of Self

You tell me it's OK, it'll be alright, but I
look up to the midnight sky, wondering
what's happening to myself—I ask why,
why life be lifin' this way? should I be
OK? and will it last as my mind goes
into overdrive!

I ask what, when, and how this happened
to me and I still don't understand why!
tell me what's happening because I
can't tell you why I feel like a deep pit,
watching the sun fall from the sky, you
say it's OK then ask me if I'm all right,
I tell you I'm so lost and confused, I
don't know what to say, so I ask you,
can you relate?

If you have all the answers, then serve
them up on my plate...

Trials, tribulations, seems like, life
comes with stipulations! looking for

an owner's manual that doesn't exist!
We do the best we can, yet the worldly
things, we still can't resist! after all,
what's wrong with a little sippy sip?

Just trying to ease the pain a little bit...

Poppin' them pills trying to have fun,
trying to escape life going on the run,
taking that my trip, dipping out for a
bit, ease my mind, or so it seems, then
I wake up from that bad ass dream,
to realize that it's really my reality,
and that gets me steamed!

Feels like I'm running in a circle, it's
hard to regain myself, getting back
to who I used to be, feeling light and
free! It's like the weight on my shoulder
is now sinking deep...

If you ask me or continue to ask me
what's wrong I wouldn't know where
to begin, so I guess that's my ultimate
sin...

So where do you begin?

I must ask you.

Did
this
sink
in...

The Wake-up call

How can you say that you're woke
while your eyes are wide open shut...

How can you say you'll lend a hand with
a fist that's so tightly shut...

Why do you shout out for help, saying
Black Lives Matter yet in the same hood
say don't snitch ...

How can you say that you want change
yet not willing to be a part of it...

Use your voice, while you still have a choice
Use your platforms to make a difference...

Woke.... Are you?

The Silence of a Masked Murderer

You showed up unexpectedly coursing
through
my veins, I didn't even know you were there
so
I went about my life the same, not knowing
how
you were pushing poison throughout my body
and inside veins...

So, I went about my life as normal, never
knowing
it will forever be changed...

This was the introduction....

Never knowing that the chill I had would
never go
away, the sneeze wasn't normal on that given
day,
or that shortness of breath would be my new
way

of life, the annoying dry cough had settled
in...

The introduction to a new reality...

How do you fight what you cannot see, how
do you
fight? how can they wield the correct weapon
when
the symptoms match so many other viruses ...

This was the introduction, that life would
never
be the same...

Unknowing that today I'd say my last
goodbye, that
today I'd have tears fall from my loved ones'
eyes,
that today would be the last time I'd see them
smile...

I never knew that
I would be
introduced

to the....
silence
of a
mass
murderer...

Matter of Facts

When you're at that point in life you want to
give up, and a sign is given to you...

When you think no one cares and then you
hear that voice say...

"I DO"...
When you are down on bended knee and you
still don't think your prayers went through...

When family and friends don't understand or
feel the depth of your pain and you don't have
the words to express or explain...

When you put on a fake smile just to make it
through...

When you've been through so many storms
and
can't take it any more...

Look to the hills from whence you'll find that the
sun (Son) has risen and shines on you once again....

There is hope, love, and life again, never give up,
never give in...

The Right to Wear My Crown

Honey if we had the time, we could talk and oh the stories
I would tell! of a joyous heaven or full of pain as I bob and
weave, while in the pits of hell, oh what a story I could tell...

Yes, honey ha! my age gives me the right to wear this crown....

In the beginning I would toil all day, and cry all night thinking
of a way out of this subservient plight, praying to give my
family the support it needs as I sit on bended knee, when
Sunday comes, I am compliant with my Lords commands
in Corinthians 11:15 to "cover my head when I come to
worship thee" and he is pleased, yes indeed...

The Lord's blessings gave me the right to wear
my crown...

My life has made a statement all its own, I
trail
blazed through history decade after decade
with
pride knowing that I am a true Queen...

My history gave me the right to wear my
crown...

As I demonstrated my Civil Rights, to
walking
up and down life's ever-changing catwalk,
don't
talk the talk if you can't walk the walk, while
remembering attitude is everything when you
enter life's heavy ring...

So yes, I hold my head up high cause I got the
right to wear my crown, I will not be cowed,
nor shall I bow out or down...

My strength gave me the right to wear my
crown...

God gave me longevity as a symbol, Life has
given me this crown filled with much
wisdom...

But time gave me the right to wear my
crown...

Be I subtle, flamboyant, graceful, or wild!
I am life and life is in me and that is the
gift that keeps on giving me the right to
wear this crown...

My whole life has given me the right to
wear my crown....

and cleanse a nation that turned a
blind eye to our blood that was
shed...

That Go Getta Mentality

What do you do when it feels like the world is closing
in on you, trying to stifle your dreams, stunt your growth?

You look around for your fam and friends, seems they've
turned into people you never really knew...

They disappear when you ask for a loan or even a ride,
time after time they push your needs to the side...

Get it....get it...

Dust it off, get it out the dirt tell yourself shit I'm gonna get
mine
start putting in that work, get on my hustle, on that
grind, they got theirs, so Imma get mines...

Get it, Get it

Ain't nothin gonna be handed to you on a silver platter, when
people see the tears they'll walk away like that don't affect

me so it doesn't matter, they'll look at you
with a smile yet have
an attitude like suck it up and move on yeah
that's a hard dose
of reality but the truth! So, what are you
gonna do?

Go Get it!

That's when you hustle, that's when you grind,
remind yourself
to leave them and all that bullshit behind, let
em' know I'm that
go getta, I'm taking what's mine...

A Hustlas' Mentality is what it takes, to
survive minute by minute
day by day,

Ask yourself...

Do you have what it takes?

The Unthinkable

Think about this for a moment
and remember...

Things that are seen cannot be unseen
Things that are heard cannot be unheard
Things that are said cannot be
unsaid...

Someone you know is crying out for help,
they are hurting beyond what your eyes
see, sometimes they lash out seemingly
for no apparent reason, and if you're not
paying attention, you could lose them...

Your words have the power to change a
mind, change an action, or even an...

OUTCOME....

Mentally exhausted

I can't move, I can't stay, I won't let you treat
me
this way, what can I do? I'm talking to a brick
wall
encased in steel a wall that has no feelings at
all...

So, you tell me how should I feel?

I'm tuggin' in a war that I can't win so why
stay?
I'm no longer allowing you to treat me this
way, a
phrase that in my head stays no matter what
price
at one time I was willing to pay, that time has
passed...

I'm exhausted...

So tired of faking the funk, tired of tiptoeing
around

the eggshells that lay on the ground that have shattered, the yolk my brain matter because nothing
I say makes a difference, you can't hear me because
you don't listen...

Exhausted, spent, lethargic, no matter how you say it,
I have no energy for this anymore, it's time to find a
space mentally and emotionally...

To be free cause....

I'm exhausted...

In my mind mentally I say to myself that I can't stay here
anymore, the more I give of myself the less I have in reserve,
my reserve is depleted; you don't care what it is that I need
or what I ever needed, so yeah...

I'm exhausted...

I am so tired of being mentally alone in what is supposed to
be my home, my Heaven, my safe place, the place that I am
supposed to be able to be me no matter what, be naked and
unafraid, mentally, physically, emotionally, and spiritually in
in the midst of a crowd, even in my own home! mentally there's
no peace for me to be me, unapologetically find yourself
apologizing for just being...

I'm exhausted...

Just...

EXHAUSTED...

In the Midnight Hour

In the daylight, it's easy to pretend and smile and laugh and believe I will see you again.

When people are gone and you're alone

by yourself, then pain makes a visit and
reality sets in, realizing I'll never see you
again....

Oh God it hurts, it hurts so bad! the
kind of pain that steals your breath
away before you scream a scream
that shakes the walls...

Yet, knowing I must endure, that's
what you would've wanted me to do,
smile that smile never let them see you
sweat, so that's what I should do, but
there are cracks in my mask that can't
be kept together not even with gorilla
glue...

The hardest part is the survivors' guilt,
the belief that I could've changed
what was already etched in stone by
God's divine will, yet again to start
thinking I could've done this, or could've
done that, anything to believe I could
change the tides trying to add more
time to your life...

I know that would be telling myself a
lie, that it would make me feel better...

Nah it won't...

That could've, would've, should've syndrome
shows up again, but the reality of I didn't
sets in, surrounded by the the desolation
of a long cold night...

The dawn of a new day leaves the
trace on a ravaged face, signs of
heartbreak all over again to be reset
at the midnight hour...

Powerless to control your feelings,
you stick them behind the steel wall
in your mind, does this work, does
does this help? does this contain the
anger that you feel at the world
When a piece of your goodness,
your Heaven is gone...

Nah it doesn't...

The clock strikes, the pain breaks
out again, the tears fall, heartbreaking
memories take over, and time flashes
before your eyes and then you look
at the hourglass that will forever be
empty...

Because your last grain of sand is
now on the other side...

In
The
Midnight
Hour

Stuck in Time

I love you but you don't know it, I always
tried my
best but at times wonder if I showed it...

I'd give you my last breath if I could take back
the
hands of time, to tell you once more that I
love you
and that you'll always be mine...

I'd give you my last breath if I could only
watch you
breathe, I'd give you a piece of my peace, just
to
have you stay and never leave, if I could look
in your
eyes and once more see the smile that lies
within, if
I could hear you say I love you, just one more
time
again...

Is wishing all of this a sin?

Would that I could erase all of the harshness
of the
words that I said, would that I could erase the
damage

that was done, wishing that I could take it all
back,
and just have you smile again...

Or I could continue to pretend...

My reality is harsh indeed, and that truth is, it
will never
again be ...

So, I....

Pretend that I am not broken, pretend my
heart is not bruised,
pretend that nothing ever happened that I
was always happy,
but then I'd lose...

I'd lose a piece of myself, that I never even
knew, I'd lose a
piece of myself as if I'm blown away in the
wind, why is it that
I'm drifting? why don't I know where to go?
my heart is telling

me I should pray, but my head it's saying I
just don't know if it
would it matter anyway ...

This world ain't built for me no more at least
not without you,
they say time would help me let you go...

And I'm sitting around here waiting for it to
do so...

I'm stuck in time, and I can't let go....

Am I the fool...

Reality Bites

This can't be my reality, yet there's no space
for
deniability, no place for procrastination, even
if I
don't want to reach the destination, time
dictates
that eventually things move on....

Nothing to indicate the stagnation that
persists to
be in existence in my mind, the circle of life is
round
for a reason, no matter how I try to fit it into
rectangular
box that is too small to encompass the
girth of my pain, yet reality persists to exist...

I don't like it, but I have no choice in the
matter...

I DON'T LIKE IT!

But time insists on moving on as if you
were never here....

In the space where you used to exist, the walls
are
now bare, the rooms are all cleared, as if you
were
never there, that pesky reality shows up
again...

I DON'T LIKE IT!

It brings an unimaginable pain; it takes the
hope away
that I'll open that door and see you again...

It's a road we'll all take eventually, and my
mind knows
this, scientific evidence proves this to be, but
in my hearts
mind, I find it hard to accept, yet that itself
doesn't change
reality...

Does it...

My mind is filled with happiness in the background that you are
no longer in pain, that you do not have to suffer, and that you
were and are at peace, and that should put my heart and mind
at ease ...

Right?

In the space that I'm in right now...

It doesn't...

I want to rage; I want to scream and fight a war thatI know I will
never win because God's will...

Will always be done....

Won't it...

My mind knows this, my heart not so much, there's a void, an

empty space, that at one time filled me with
so much love, happiness
and joy, my cup runneth over, then reality
shows up again in the dawn
of a new day...

Ha, in my arrogance I thought I had it all
figured out, plans regarding
time that I didn't know I didn't have, I guess
the joke was on me, maybe
there was something there that I overlooked
in my minds eye that I
could not see....

That pesky ...

R. E . A. L. I . T. Y

B. I. T. E. S

Again...

MASK ON / MASK OFF

I get the news and can't believe that this is really happening

to me, I pray for the strength to see this through, at war with
the feelings of what I think as God's betrayal and thinking
thoughts that to you may seem disloyal as if I'm an unbeliever
but still, I smile and pretend all is well cause I'm just not ready
to tell you yet...

Mask on

I love you so much that you'll never know the pain I'm going
through, no matter what I'll just suck it up, just to spend a few
more moments with you...

Mask on....

How are you doing? I'm doing fine, after the sessions I feel a horrible
mess, to see your smile I'll finish all these damn tests, through

my pain I'm lying, and in my heart, I'm crying
but for you, I'll fight
on through...

Mask on...

The weight goes first, then the hair, in the
mirror I sit for hours and
stare, I joke around a little bit, yet I'm weary
and full of a thirst that
I can't seem to quench I see the worry in your
eyes, so I ask the nurse,
Can we finish this?

I'm through...

The tests are back, what could the results be?
I've done everything
the doctor's have asked of me, outside I'm
calm and cool, while praying
to God if he'll once again pull me through....

Mask on...

The mass has grown, or has it gone away this
is your story to tell, your
moment in time, sad to say my Mom didn't
make it but I'm her legacy,
1 of five to allow her light to shine, she
survives through my siblings
and in me....

This was her story...

Mask Off...

ForeverLand

While walking in the garden with the Lord
one day he
said to Mother this phrase" I have given you
the time
you asked, now it's time for your pain to pass."
Mother replied "well Lord whatever will my
children do?
The time I asked was to prepare them for
when my time
on this earth was through" ....

The Lord replied but my dear YOU are my child too, and
YOU did the best you could do, as I can no longer allow
you to bear this pain that from them you continue to hide
night after night and day after day, you must trust in me
of them to take care and know that I will always be there,
especially in times of sorrow, trials, loss and with it the
terrible pain, know that one day they WILL smile again...

Be still my child; know that I am GOD, able to heal all wounds,
and ease all pain know his in your heart and soul to be true,
now come my child, come let us take the forever walk to the
place I have prepared for you....

Mother hesitated for a moment letting it all sink in, she looked
back and blew a kiss to the family she loved so very much and
will surely miss, she then turned to take the Lord's hand with a
big smile saying "Father you already have my soul, now into
your keeping I give my heart to thee, for they are all I have,
these blessings once given to me ...

She left this world with a peaceful expression on her face as she
walked with her Father to her forever place ....

LOVE YOU FOREVER MORE MOMMA... FOREVER MORE......

Change is Coming

Something, something, just ain't right, it feels
like one day we
were perfect, now all we do is argue and fight
...

There's something I need to say, this is
something that I need
to do, yet every time I get close, you say
there's something more
important you need to do, how can we discuss
this like grown adults,
without all the back-and-forth, can't you see
that's getting old and
gives us no results ...

It's Time for Change...

How can I believe a word that comes out of
your mouth when every
time we talk, we argue, now what's that all
about...

You sit there and point out my flaws, yet
perfection has never been
perfected by any human being, now you do an
honest self reflection,
and see exactly what I mean ...

Narcissistic behavior at its finest, ha you
really think you were bestowed
this power...

There's something I need to say, yes, it's
something I need to do, but every
time I try to communicate the importance of
this, there's something more
important to...

You ...

They say communication is the key, but I say
it's really...

Self...

Discovery ...

BreaKer oF tHe StoRm

They said her trials would make her bow
down and
kneel before a mere man...

She said NEVER that, attached a splint to her
back ignoring
the pain...
They whispered "she'll never make it" when
she stumbled...
She yelled to the heavens "I got this" and
made it through...

They said the storm had come to break her, to
wipe her out....
She said didn't you know....

I AM Anointed BY the water...

WATER IS LIFE....

Therefore...

I AM

THE

STORM....

BREAKER....

It could NEVA

BREAK...

ME...

Today's Heroes... Tomorrow's Saviors

You ease the trauma that has swept a nation,
you've
given HEROES new definition, a new face
and for this...

Thank You ...

To so many you've helped sustain them
mentally when
they couldn't gather their thoughts,
emotionally when
they didn't know whether to scream or cry,
and physically
when the body was unable to function as it
should...

Thank you...

To many you've been the information
highway, the bridge

connecting a nation of families and friends,
taking the
extra-steps, while making so many sacrifices
without
thought, your tiredness and weariness left
unspoken,
yet you continue to push through....

Fighting through your own fears to ease those
that are
terrified of the unknown, you are the calm in
the eye of
the storm...

Thank You...

You've told the truth, when you could lie,
risking much to
save a life...

Thank You...

To so many you are the light at the end of the
tunnel, to so

many you fix the broken and make them new,
yet still too
many you are their only companion when the
journey
on this earth is through, this is truly the
greatest gift to
families unable to see their loved ones
transitioning to
the other side...

NOTE: Today's Heroes... Tomorrow's Saviors
This poem reflects just a few words of
appreciation for the unsung
heroes that are in the Medical and Healthcare
field, the First
Responders as well as Essential Workers
risking their
lives everyday for something more than just a
paycheck...

Please know that you made a difference...

Thank You...

Chameleon Emotions

When does perfection become imperfection?
When does trying to give love and
consideration
become dependency wrapped in despondency
searching for liberation?

When and how did the tides change, hmmm I
guess nothing ever really remains the same...

When does giving your all to someone mean
losing yourself, becoming so wrapped up in
that person, so lost and confused that the
very concept of the word "ME" is really all
about you...

Where did the disrespect and neglect come
from, with so much discourtesy, when did
you stop seeing...

ME...

When does wanting to be in the presence

and basking in their very essence, the
essence of the one you love become
smothering and a cloying need of space?

When does a basic conversation start feeling
like an attack with every word a direct hit?

For every question, there's a lie for an answer,
getting the truth is like pulling teeth or
finding
a cure for cancer, the topic of the
conversation
toxic, your own home it feels like you're the
stranger in a house with four walls and a door
but you can't lock it...

Wanting to run, but for closure feeling you
gotta
stay, feeling they are the only one for you and
it's
too much time invested in, to walk away....

So, at times justification is found to ....

STAY....

How does one recognize the person within, when the changes that have taken place were so subtle, how does one shake the feeling that their very own body double is staring back from the mirror...

When did the changes come...
How were the signs missed....

This is Me! the being that you were to love always...

Me that you promised to cherish for all days...

Me that always held you down...
Me who you won't miss...

Until I'm not around...

Changes coming soon from
a
Me

you
use
to

know...

Forgiveness

Lord, forgive me in advance, I'm so
tired of suffering, I'm so tired of the
pain, I no longer understand what it
is in the end that I will gain...

Here I am on bended knees, eyes
full of tears begging if you'll please,
just please take it all away for I don't
know how much more I can take,
just ready to give it all up...

Today...

I know they say trials and tribulations
will always be our bedfellows and
sometimes our friends, but I have
to ask how long this will be 'cause
right now, I'm at my wit's end...

Judgments, jealousy, envy, struggles,
and strife seem to be the author of
my life, I don't know if in a past life or

lives I've caused others so much pain, but in this life, I guess it sets all the records straight....

If I am to be forgiven, I give my life to you for they say that I am unworthy, but I know that is untrue, they say to take your own life is to do so in vain, for hell is destination and entry to heaven never to be gained....

For He gives me wisdom when I am foolish and when I am weary, he showed me what to do, glory when I ask for grace, for I am blessed to see his face...

So, I'm no longer committed to do this thing called suicide, for I've found the Lord and he is the light of my life, so I guess I'll bless this world with my presence a bit longer 'cause that makes me stronger and when I'm weak picking me up dusting off my feet now I see...

I am forgiven unconditionally...

SeLf Love

Stop playing the blame game with yourself,
time to let go
and move on, yet never forgetting the lessons
you learned...

That's how you move forward ...

The past and its mistakes are what you did,
not who you are,
don't allow them to define person you are
today, time is precious,
so don't waste it or the energy to
continuously beat yourself up...

Through the process you've learned your
lessons and earned wisdom
that will prevent you from making the same
mistakes again, you now
know better so do better...

The lessons learned well, you now have a
chance to apply them and

correct your behaviors depend on how you
look at it, either continue
to be stuck on past mistakes, and allow them
to hold you back or turn
your mistakes into learning opportunities and
bounce back stronger
than ever before...

Forgive yourself for past mistakes, no matter
how big or small, time
is short and waits for no one...

The choice is yours...

Choose wisely ...

Growth

I had to cut some old branches off my tree,
can't keep feeding my
roots with food that's not meant for me,
won't keep watering my
roots with polluted energy ...

I have to be who I'm meant to be, and some
won't make it on this
new journey with me so they'll fall on the
weigh side, gotta let
the already dead weight die never to be
revived....

Time to use this lancet to allow lightning to
cauterize the wounds
in my heart and time to stop using faucet
water on my lawn and
allow the rain to rejuvenate dead roots,

Let go so the blessings can pour forth and
overflow...

Yet remember...

To whom much is given much is expected...

The Hourglass.... A Life of Time

It goes from us in years
It goes from us in months
It goes from us in weeks
It goes from us in days
It goes from us in hours
It goes from us in minutes
It's GONE from us in mere
seconds...

TIME....

The one thing that we take for
granted
The one thing that we often ignore
The one thing we are gifted
But the very thing is taken away....

TIME...

It waits for no one, yet we waste it
everyday, for every second, minute,

hour and day spent on past hurts and
at times imagined pains...

Don't put off for tomorrow, what you
can say and do today, for when time runs
out for a loved one, what's left unsaid is
what's regretted day after day....

They can no longer physically hear or feel
whatever it is you have or need to say...

The hourglass is ticking, so what have you
been missing....

TIME...
You think you have
so
much
of
it
until
it's
gone ...